UNDERSTANDING
GOD'S CALL

THE JOURNEY TOWARDS KNOWING YOUR TRUE SELF

COLIN **SHILSTON**

real stories. real hope.

wildsidepublishing.com

Published by Colin Shilston in association with Wild Side Publishing
www.wolnz.org | www.wildsidepublishing.com

Cover design and copywriting Ray & Janet Curle, WSP
Text layout Janet Curle, WSP, www.wildsidepublishing.com

Cataloguing in Publication Data:
Title: Understanding God's Call

ISBN: 978-0-473-56104-8 (paperback)
        978-0-473-56300-4 (epub)

Subjects: Inspiration, Spirituality, Body Soul Spirit, Christian, Non-Fiction, New Zealand, Mission, Christian Living

First New Zealand printing, January 2021
International listing, Ingram Spark February 2021

CONTENTS

ENDORSEMENTS

Don Barry | **Senior Leader, Gateway Church, Hamilton, New Zealand:**

It has often been said that there are three requirements required for a fulfilling life: a clear sense of personal identity, a deep sense of life's meaning and a strong sense of purpose and mission. Colin's powerful little book speaks to all three.

This is a book that all new believers {and old one's for that matter} would benefit greatly from reading. Too many of us have stumbled on the truths outlined in the book much later in our lives and often taught to us by virtue of bitter experiences when, had we been in possession of a book like this, we might have come to grasp them much earlier, and perhaps, much easier. The book does not profess to offer an exact 'roadmap' {beware those that do!} and yet it nonetheless is packed with wisdom and insight as to how God fashions a man or woman of God. I found it illuminating and encouraging and I'm sure you will too.

Vic Francis | **Pastor Shore Vineyard, Auckland, NZ and Principal Vineyard Bible College:**

The gap between a glib, *"God loves you and has a great plan for your life"* and personally discovering both that love, and that plan can actually be a chasm.

In *Understanding God's Call,* Colin Shilston goes deep into the 'calls' of scripture to discover what God's call actually is, what it looks and feels like, and how to discern it for yourself. In doing so, Colin is both scholarly and human, and certainly never glib, in providing a foundation for the seeker to go deeper into the journey of discovering God's call. This book won't give you all the answers, and doesn't try to, but it may well inspire you on the journey of discovering the answers for yourself.

INTRODUCTION

What does it mean to be called by God? Is this something to be attained by a few spiritual giants, or is it something that we should all be able to know and walk in? Are there seasons in the journey of pursuing God's call, and what does this look like in everyday life? Is it possible to understand our lives, even our everyday lives, in the context of God's call?

I and many of the people I have encountered in my years of Christian ministry, have wrestled with these questions. James Fowler once wrote, "We do not live long, or well without meaning,"[1] and so the search to discover God's call grows out of a deep human need to understand and engage in lives of significance. Consequently, the struggle to articulate and actualise that call causes a deep pain for some, particularly those who see their life passing and feel somehow that they have not fully understood or connected meaningfully with their call.

---

1 James W. Fowler, Becoming Adult, Becoming Christian, Adult Development and the Christian Faith (San Francisco, Josey-Bass, 2000), 39

Sometimes, it is just easier not to see life in those terms. We zone out to meaning or pay it lip-service, and just get on with the business of living life as it comes. People easily can develop a dualistic mindset where they can speak and sing and believe of divine purpose on Sundays, but for the rest of the week they just revert to 'life as usual' in their work and personal lives. These two worlds can co-exist, yet deep down there is a yearning that somehow all of life could be understood and connected to the bigger picture of God's purpose and call for us.

Churches have not always been so helpful in this. Inadvertently, they can sometimes send confused messages as to what God's call constitutes and how it is outworked. At other times, the call to 'walk in the calling of God', given explicitly from the pulpit or implicitly as a cultural value, has actually intensified the pain for those who feel that they have not yet discerned their call and who live lives that don't seem to show any proof of being ordered around, or connected to, a specific purpose or call.

At other times, people may have sensed or engaged with what they perceived as a call from the Lord, only to find that it does not play out as they expected. I have walked with many people who find themselves in this place, and it can be very disheartening and disorientating. Questions like, "Did I hear God?" or "Did I do wrong?" arise. Even more so, "How can I move forward from this place with confidence?".

Writing to the Christians in Ephesus, the apostle Paul records his prayer for them. In Ephesians one verse eighteen Paul wrote that he prayed that,

"The eyes of your heart may be enlightened that you may know what is the hope of your calling."

What Paul is praying for is not information, but enlightenment to come to them. Enlightenment is the coming of light by which things come into clarity. This is more a function of the heart than the head, which is why Paul prays for the eyes of their heart to be enlightened. My prayer is that as you read these pages, you will not just receive information but will also have moments of enlightenment, a heart experience where clarity comes, and confusion is dispelled.

As a result, you will have an increased capacity to know the hope of your calling and your ability to look upon your world and life with hope-filled eyes will increase. This is not a worldly hope, which depends on things turning out how you wished. Rather, it is an inner disposition that understands the purposes God has for you and is able to discern how these purposes are being outworked in the midst of your ups and downs, trials and triumphs, and day-to-day realities.

On this journey, I will start by using the Bible to define what a call is, and what is the foundation of your call; that is, the things that call must rest on. Then, I will progress to look at the lives of some biblical characters and what you can learn from them about how call operates in their lives. In this way, the book acts like an art gallery. As you pause to look at each piece (chapter), your engagement with the lives of each one is intended to provide a context where the Holy Spirit can bring truth to you about your life and journey. The book acts also like an exercise track, designed not to take you to a specific place, but to build your strength and fitness so that you can better run your own race. I will talk a bit more about these metaphors and how our call works as part of God's jigsaw puzzle at the end of the book.

But for now, like all things you must start not at the end, but at the beginning. We will do this by asking, "What is a call?" and, "What are the foundations on which call is built?" Foundations constitute what you truly believe about God, yourself, and the world. It is on this foundation that your sense of purpose and call stands. Having understood what call is, it is then prudent to make sure that your foundation is well built.

UNDERSTANDING CALL AND IT'S FOUNDATION

Before we begin this journey, it is vital that we have a clear understanding of what a call is. In the Christian sense I see a call as being a specific divine grace to a particular purpose. Examples of this would be Paul's call to be an apostle to the Gentiles, or John the Baptist's call to prepare the way of the Lord.

Throughout the Old and New Testament, we see people receiving various calls that connect their lives to the outworking and development of God's plans and purposes.

In the first verse of the book of Romans Paul introduces himself as one "called to be an apostle.[1]" The Greek word for call Paul uses here is *kletos* from the noun *klesis* which the Vines Word book says "is always used in the New Testament of that calling, the origin, nature and destiny of which are heavenly.[2]"

---

1   Romans 1:1
2   Vines Complete Expository Dictionary of Old and New Testament

In like manner in the book of Ephesians Paul refers his ministry as a grace that was given to him.[3] A calling will involve an empowering (grace) to fulfil a particular function, in a specific place, or to a particular people, as designated by God. It is in Paul's words from Ephesians chapter two verse ten the "works that He prepared in advance for us to do."

However, while the call itself is specific, there is a wider journey of formation and discovery of that call. We will see this in the lives of the people we examine. For them, and us, faith is needed to walk this journey towards the revelation and outworking of that call.

A vital part of that process will be the building of the foundation in our lives on which a call can rest on. When building anything, the first thing you build is the foundation because everything else will either stand or fall depending on its strength. If you are to understand the call of God, you must first give attention to the foundations on which it is built. On my journey, many times when I thought that I was building something I realised that God was actually building a foundation in my life which only later would be built upon.

Like most things in Christianity, the foundation on which you build, is a faith statement, a belief that

Words, Editors: W.E Vine, William White, Meryll F. Unger, Thomas Nelson Inc, 1985, 87

3   Ephesians 3:2

God is shaping your life to the end of fulfilling His good purposes. This is what the apostle Paul was talking about when he wrote:

"For we are God's workmanship, created in Christ Jesus, to do good works which God prepared in advance for us to do.[4]"

This Scripture squarely attacks the modern myth of self-actualisation. The belief that I am responsible to make something of myself. This shifts the central axis, declaring that we are God's workmanship. The prime mover in this work is God, not you. The Greek word for workmanship, *poiema*, focuses on what God is making, not on my self-effort to become something. This is the foundation stone on which you must stand. This is the faith position that states that God is working to shape your life so that you will achieve the things that He prepared in advance for you to do.

To this you might ask, "But how are the complex relationships, challenges, successes, failures, tragedies, and triumphs of my life related to the God's call?" This is where examining the Biblical characters can help us because the people in the bible are very human, with jobs and families, hopes and talents, frailties and frustrations. Although they lived in different historical and cultural contexts, they display the way in which God calls, shapes, and uses

---

4   Ephesians 2:10

people to fulfil His purposes in specific times and places.

Later on, we will examine some Biblical characters and look at what we can learn from their journeys.

The position of faith outlined in Ephesians two verse ten, is also stated in Psalm twenty-one verse one where David, speaking out from the foundational truth of his life, wrote, "The Lord is my shepherd I shall not want." This is a radical statement of trust. Here, David states his belief that God is faithful to shepherd his life to the fulfilling of His purpose. If you do not believe this, then you will be the one doing the shepherding, trying to bring about the desired outcome. I spent many years in various ways trying to bring about a result that would satisfy my ego needs and desire for significance, only to discover that God, not me, is the Good Shepherd. Only He can lead us to "life in all its fullness.[5]" If you have this faith as a foundation, then you will be able to enter a place of peace. You will not perhaps understand everything, but you will have a deep trust that God, the Good Shepherd is about His work, and you can rest in that. David calls this the place of "green pastures and still waters". In the New Testament, the writer of Hebrews, says "Now we who have believed enter that rest.[6]"

5   John 10:10
6   Hebrews 4:3

Once you have entered the rest that comes from faith, then God can do the work of restoring your soul.[7] This involves removing the fear and anxiety operating within us around our security, identity, and significance. Deep within many of us is the core belief that our identity comes out of what we have and what we achieve. Without our achievements and attainments, we stand naked and ashamed before ourselves, the world, and ultimately God, and this is too much for us to bear. We, like Adam and Eve in the garden of Eden after the Fall, cannot bear our nakedness. Often, our first response, like Adam and Eve, is to cover up by gathering things around us (works, achievements, possessions, and relationships) seeking to cover our nakedness, avoiding shame, and making us feel secure.

In contrast, before the Fall, we are told that Adam and Eve were "naked and unashamed.[8]" I believe they were able to exist in this state for two reasons. Firstly, their identity lay not in what they did, but who they were, and secondly, they were able to live under the Word God spoke over them.

First and foremost, they knew their identity was as image bearers of God. In this way they were created to display His glory. This image of God in us was distorted by sin at the Fall of mankind. However, the good news is that as a Christian this image

7   Psalm 23:3
8   Genesis 2:25

has now been fully restored to you in Christ. This is because Christ, who is "the image of the invisible God,[9]" now lives in you, thus restoring you to the role of image bearer. One of the early church fathers, Athanasius wrote "So, the Word of God came himself, in order that he being the image of the Father (cf. Col 1.15), the human being "in the image" might be recreated[10]."

Secondly, I believe they were able to be naked and unashamed because they lived under the word that God had spoken over them. In Genesis one verse thirty-one we read, "And God saw all that He had made, and it was very good." The ability to live by this word will banish shame from you and enable you to walk naked and unashamed. If you are able to know that in Christ, God looks at you and declares your life good, then shame is taken from your life.

For many years I have not lived out of this truth and have struggled to walk in the freedom Jesus came to give us[11] Jesus said in John eight verse thirty-two, "you will know the truth, and the truth will set you free". To know this truth requires that you grow in the knowledge of how God sees you. I thought that God viewed me as I viewed myself, but

9   Colossians 1:15
10   Saint Athanasius, (Translation and introduction by John Beir) *On the Incarnation*, New York, St Vladimir's Seminary Press, 2011, Kindle, Loc 922
11   Galatians 5:1

I was wrong. I well remember a time when I learned that something that I had worked at for years had failed. In that moment, God spoke to me through Psalm eighteen verse nineteen,

"He brought me to a spacious place; he rescued me because he delighted in me."

The knowledge that God delighted in me, revolutionised my heart and drew me in love towards Him. I began to see myself as He sees me. Not as a failure, but as a delight.

"But wait!" I hear you say, "Doesn't the Bible declare me a sinner worthy of condemnation?" No, actually it does not. It declares that your human nature, broken by sin, is hostile to God. Paul says this in Romans eight verse seven,

"The sinful mind is hostile to God. It does not submit to God's law, nor can it do so."

But in Romans seven verse twenty-two he wrote, "For in my inner being I delight to do God's law." And so, Paul separates out the two, writing, "As it is, it is no longer myself who do it, but sin living in me.[12]"

Paul was able to affirm himself as good, and sin as bad, and separate the two. Unless you are able to do this, you will always be held captive by shame. Paul confidently declares in Romans eight verse one there to be "now no condemnation for those in Christ Jesus." When you trust in Christ, sin has

---

12   Romans 7:17

been named and dealt with, and you have been redeemed and set free. God declares once again over your life that you are "very good". It is the "accuser of the brethren,[13]" Satan, not God, that seeks to bring you under bondage to shame and fear, and keep you from being glorious. It is Jesus, who calls His followers the "light of the world,[14]" and encourages them not to hide that light from the world by putting it under a 'bowl' of shame.[15]

Once you have trusted that God is your shepherd, the one who is fashioning your life that you may walk in the "works that He prepared in advance for you to do,[16]" you come into the rest of faith. Then you can embrace the work of Him who is restoring your soul, so that you may be free of shame and anxiety.

My experience is that this is a progressive work in us, but as it happens, the next line of Psalm twenty—three comes into play: "And guides my path in righteousness for His Name sake[17]". Actually, God has been guiding the path the whole way, but from the position of faith and inner peace, the foundation is now set on which God can build a call.

We see this back in Genesis too. Only after God had established people as His image bearers and proclaimed the word over them that they were very

13   Revelation 12:10
14   Matthew 5:14
15   Matthew 5:15
16   Ephesians 2:10
17   Psalm 23:3

good, did God then give them the specific call which is recorded in Genesis two verse fifteen,

"The Lord God took the man and put him in the garden of Eden to work it and take care of it."

Therefore, whatever call (or specific work) God gives you, must rest upon the base of these two other things, the understanding of the glory of your identity as an image bearer of God, and believing the word that you are good and pleasing to Him.

A similar pattern is observed in the life of Jesus. At His baptism before Jesus starts His ministry, God says in Luke three verse twenty-two,

"This is my Son, whom I love; with him I am well pleased."

Here we see the same pattern: first Jesus is declared a son—that is an image bearer of the Father—and then that He is loved and is pleasing to God—in other words 'very good.' Once this is established, we move on to Luke four verse eighteen where Jesus now declares His call,

"The Spirit of the Sovereign Lord is on me, because he has anointed me to preach good news to the poor. He has sent me to proclaim freedom for the prisoners and recovery of sight for the blind, to release the oppressed, to proclaim the year of the Lord's favour."

Jesus knows this as His call, yet before he steps into it, he already has in place his identity as an image bearer of God, and the knowledge that he is loved and pleasing to God.

The Sign of the Sabbath

As I mentioned earlier, it is easy for you to see your value and ability to please God tied up with fruitful service. Growing up in a culture where you are valued for your utilitarian value—what you can make, achieve, or consume—it is easy to see why this is a common mistake. Being raised in this culture means that this is the paradigm that is most natural for you to adopt.

Even within the church I found it easy to feel that I was affirmed and valued for what I could contribute, and therefore could embrace a belief that my usefulness was equated with my value.

I see a parallel in the Bible for the Israelites in the time of Exodus. The Israelites has spent 400 years in Egypt working as servants and then slaves to the Egyptians. Certainly, as slaves, they were only valued in terms of what they could produce. However, when God delivered them out of Egypt, God established in the law the Sabbath, a day in which they were instructed not to work. In Exodus thirty-one verse thirteen God says,

"You must observe my Sabbaths. This will be a sign between me and you, for generations to come."

The Hebrew word for sign means "something by which a group or person is characteristically marked.[18]" So, what was the characteristic that the Sabbath was pointing to? In observing the Sabbath, the Israelites were prophetically declaring that they were not slaves and that the value of their lives was not determined by the work they did but was found in their relationship to God. This observance was necessary to break the Israelites out of their slave mentality so that they could work *from* identity and significance, rather than *for* it.

In the New Testament, in Matthew eleven verse twenty-eight, Jesus speaks directly to those who fashioned by the work-based culture of the world, have become 'weary and burdened.' He calls them to come to Him, and He will 'give them rest.' The Greek word used here for rest is *anapousis* and Vines Dictionary says that this is the constant word used in the Septuagint (The Greek translation of the Old Testament) for the Sabbath[19]. Jesus says He will give us Sabbath.

For many years I let work define who I was, and saw my value being tied up with what I could produce. I needed to allow God to lead me out of Egypt (that is slavery to the work bound pattern of this world) and let Jesus give me both freedom and rest.

18   Vines Complete Expository Dictionary of Old and New Testament
      Words. Thomas Nelson Publishers, Nashville Tennessee, 229
19   Ibid., 529

The ability to do this is actually a prophetic sign that you are no longer slaves (that is given value from what you produce) but that your identity and value come to you through your connection to God as image bearers of Him.

Once this is established, Jesus then goes on to say in verse twenty-nine, "Take my yoke upon you". Having entered into this rest, now you are able to receive the yoke (that is the call to work) because you are rested in the knowledge that your identity and value are found not in your work, but in your connection to Christ.

Conclusion

So, I learned an important truth: God is already at work in my life fashioning me to walk in His call, the works that He prepared in advance for me to do. This is true also for you. I believe that He wants you by faith to rest in this truth.

As you do, God will begin to restore your soul from the fear and anxiety that His call on your life may not be realised. Consequently, you will be released from the modern mania of needing to strive for significance and from the fear of somehow missing the mark. You can confidently declare, as Paul does in first Thessalonians five verse twenty-four,

"The One who calls you is faithful and He will do it."

Also, once you recognise your identity as an image bearer of God and receive His word over your life that you are good and pleasing to Him, then you are no longer driven by fear to clothe yourself with achievements and attainments to justify your existence. Unfortunately, much of religion is also energised by working to please God, instead of resting in His love. I am reminded of Jesus' words in Luke twelve verse thirty-two,

"Do not be afraid, little flock. Your Father has been pleased to give you the Kingdom."

When God brings you out of the culture that has taught you that you are valuable only through achievement, He gives you Sabbath (that is rest), so that you can work from the place of significance, rather than working to achieve it. All of this constitutes the basis or foundations of your life, and it is on this foundation, that any call or work of God can be built.

Foundations are great, but you can't live in a foundation. In fact, it only exists for what will be placed on it. To move on from here, we will turn to look at the lives of people in the Bible who fulfilled a call of God. Often, we find that God's word comes to us with flesh on, as a lived reality rather than a theoretical framework. As we turn now to look at the life of Abram, you will face questions like, Are you prepared to walk a journey where the destination is not stated at the beginning? Are you prepared to become a pilgrim, and if so, what characteristics do you need to embrace this journey?

Together we will see ways in which Abram's journey is descriptive of the key elements of the pilgrim's life.

ABRAM

"This hill though high I covent ascend;
The difficulty will not me offend;
For I perceive the way of life lies here.
Come, pluck up, heart;
let's neither faint nor fear."

John Bunyan (Pilgrim's Progress)

In Genesis twelve we find what is titled, "The call of Abram." It reads:

"The Lord said to Abram, "Leave your country, your people and your father's household and go to the land I will show you"."

Here, you find an aspect of Abram's call that may resonate with your journey. This is that although Abram's call is definite, it's not specific. The Lord does not say "Go to this specific land," rather, we hear him saying "Go to the land that I will show you."

This can be encouraging if you find yourself on a journey which seems (at least at the outset) not to have a specific destination. For Abram, a God encounter sets him on a journey, at which point he becomes a pilgrim, someone moving towards an as-yet unknown destination.

The writer of Psalm eighty-four wrote,

"Blessed are those whose strength is in you, who have set their hearts on pilgrimage.[1]"

The psalms are often written in a form called Hebrew parallelism, where the second line re-states the first in a variated form. Thus, in this case, the parallelism makes a connection between pilgrimage and having our strength in God. Pilgrimage by its nature requires you to be a person in process or transition, moving from one place to another. Such a journey makes us reliant on God's strength, not our own, allowing the Lord to be our shepherd and trusting that He will shepherd our journey towards the destination He has in mind.

Embracing the pilgrim journey will also require you to adopt a posture that can handle change. Jesus used the metaphor of wineskins in the New Testament to show that only new wineskins (which are flexible and able to change) are of use for new wine. Pursuing God's call will require you to be flexible and open to the new wine of new ideas and experiences.

---

1   Psalm 84:5

This may require that you leave behind things that once defined and validated you. The first part of Abram's call is all about leaving, "Leave your country, your people and your father's household". To Abram, this means that which is known and familiar. He knows this country, and therefore is able to navigate it by his knowledge. However, the road to engaging with God's call will take him to unfamiliar places that will require new learning. You may not have to move to a new country to follow God's call (although you may) but regardless, you will at times have to farewell ways of thinking and being to embrace new ways on the journey of walking out God's call. It is possible if you hold too tightly to what you have, God cannot lead you forwards into your call. God will always maintain our freedom. Had Abram refused to leave the land of his fathers, he would never have discovered the land of promise.

In 2017 God called my wife and I to leave our jobs and home country to spend two years as pilgrims in Canada. We left New Zealand with two suitcases and a guitar. The focus of this journey was for me to do a master's degree in ministry at St Stephen's University in New Brunswick, but of course God had much more in mind than just study.

Being on this journey required us to gain our strength from God. Along the way we encountered new places, and people, but also learned much about ourselves and became open to new ideas and teachings. Before leaving God gave me the Scripture Jeremiah thirty-three verse three, "Call to me and I will answer you and tell you great and unsearchable things you do not know." I discovered that there are things that you can learn on the pilgrim journey, that you previously did not know and could not have known outside of walking that journey.

For us, this also involved leaving our family and children for two years. For Abram this required leaving "his people, and his father's household". You will discover that pursuing your call may not only cost you, but also cost the people around you. People may not understand you and may even oppose you on this path. This is why Jesus was so clear in the New Testament that even family relationships must come second to our obedience to God's call.[2]

So, why would you move from the place of security to insecurity? From the place of knowing, to a place of unknowing? Why would you risk walking away from all that to follow a call that is yet undefined?

Regarding Abram, the writer of the New Testament book of Hebrews addresses some of these questions saying,

"By faith, Abram, when called to go to a place that he would later receive as his inheritance, obeyed

---

2   Matthew 10:37

and went, even though he did not know where he was going.[3]"

Later in verses fourteen and sixteen he wrote,

"...admitting they were foreigners and strangers on earth... they were longing for a better country—a heavenly one."

At the base of Abram's motivation, and those who like him embrace the way of the pilgrim, is a profound dissatisfaction with the world (country) of their own, and a deep longing for a 'better country'. Although this present country can offer you, at some level comfort, affirmation, and a sense of place and identity, there is also a sense that it is deeply flawed and that God is calling you onwards to something that reflects and manifests a better country, a heavenly one. It is this deep-seated dissatisfaction that energises people to leave behind these other things and become a pilgrim in search of this higher reality.

In 2016 I travelled around Europe, the UK, the middle East and America as a pilgrim, seeking to connect with places, people and communities, that displayed aspects of this heavenly reality in ways that would shape and inspire me. This laid the foundation for what would later be an extended period away from New Zealand, as God continued to draw my wife and I along this path, towards a higher and greater reality.

---

3   Hebrews 11:8

In the New Testament, this heavenly country is what is referred to as the Kingdom of God. Jesus, in His famous Sermon on the Mount, encourages His followers to seek after this reality as a first priority.[4] This is an invitation to the pilgrim way. There is a cost to embracing this which may mean you becoming "aliens and strangers on earth.[5]" This is because your heart yearns toward the "city with foundations, whose architect and builder is God."[6] To do this, you will indeed need the strength of God which He gives to those who set their hearts on pilgrimage.

Aspects of the Journey

In chapter twelve, Abram continues his pilgrim journey taking him to various places. It records that he stopped at Shechem; from there pitched his tent in the hills between Bethel and Ai; then he heads towards the Negev; and then it records that he heads down to Egypt because of a famine. Those of us on the pilgrim's journey can learn something from these places that God leads Abram because each of them can represent aspects of the journey of call.

---

4   Matthew 6:33
5   Hebrews 11:13
6   Hebrews 11:10

Shechem—God's Word

Shechem represents the Word of God and this is the first place Abram camps. Shechem appears later in the Bible in Joshua's time,

"On that day Joshua made a covenant for the people, and there at Shechem he drew up for them decrees and laws. And Joshua recorded these things in the Book of the Law of God.[7]"

Shechem was also the place where the people committed themselves to the Word God had given them.[8]

You will not understand or step into the call of God without embracing His Word. For Abram this was the spoken words he received. We too receive words from the Lord as we read the Bible. Jesus said in Matthew four verse four, "Man does not live by bread alone, but by every word that proceeds from the mouth of God." When we go to the Bible with the expectation of receiving the words from His mouth, God will meet you at your own 'Shechem'. The writer of Psalm one hundred and nineteen experienced this. In this epic psalm he writes things like, "The unfolding of your words gives me light;[9]" and "Direct my footsteps according to Your word;[10]"

---

7   Joshua 24:25
8   Joshua 24:27
9   Psalm 119:130
10   Psalm 119:133

and the well-known verse, "Your word is a lamp to my feet and a light to my path.[11]"

Early in my pilgrimage, while reading Psalm one hundred and nineteen, I experienced a verse that seemed to come from His mouth to me. Verse one hundred and two says,

"I have not departed from your laws, for You Yourself have taught me."

In that moment, I felt God saying that if I would continue to come to His Word, that He Himself would teach me. In that day, I committed to continuing to open His Word with an expectant heart, because He said that He Himself would teach me. My experience is that God has been very faithful to do what He promised.

In Joshua chapter twenty-four we read in verse twenty-six,

"Then he (Joshua) took a large stone and set it up there (Shechem) under the Oak tree near the Holy Place of the Lord."

The stone was there for people to return to so that they might remember the covenant words of God. It is good to set up stones of remembrance around the words that God has given you so you may return to them and remember. That is why I wrote down the things that God showed me, so that they may become as stones of remembrances that I can

---

11   Psalm 119:105

return to. We also discover that Shechem is the place of authority. Shechem in Hebrew means literally 'shoulder,' and in Isaiah nine verse six we read,

"For to us a child is born, to us a son is given, and the government will be on his shoulders."

This child Isaiah refers to is Jesus, who in John chapter one verse one is called the "The Word." The authority of God (God's government) rests upon the shoulders of the Word of God.

It is important for you to know this, because walking in the call of God will be opposed and resisted by the devil. You see this illustrated in Luke chapter four. The moment Jesus begins to walk in His calling, the devil is right there to oppose Him. However, Jesus meets each attack with the Word of God, countering the devil with the words "It is written.[12]" To walk in the call of God, you will have to know what it is to carry the authority of the Word of God and counter the attacks of the enemy with, "It is written."

Between the Hills of Bethel and Ai — The church

The next place recorded that Abram camped was "in the hills between Bethel and Ai.[13]" Genesis twenty-eight records Jacob's significant encounter with

---

12   Luke 4:4, 8
13   Genesis 12:8

God at Bethel. Here, in a dream, he sees the angels of God ascending and descending on a ladder, and on waking he says,

"Surely the Lord was in this place... how awesome is this place. This is none other than the house of God.[14]"

Living out the call of God will involve you connecting with the house of God, which, in New Testament times is the church. Peter refers to this in his first letter when he wrote,

"and you also, like living stones are being built into a spiritual house.[15]"

Like a house, every part must be connected and related to the rest of the house. Only in this context, does each part find its meaning.

Genesis twelve verse eight says that Abram camped between Bethel and Ai. Joshua seven records Ai as the place that the Israelites attacked but were defeated because of Achan who had sinned by taking some of the 'devoted things' (things that were meant to have been destroyed) and hiding them in his tent. As a result, the people of God suffered defeat in this place. Being connected to a people means you not only share in their benefits but also you share their mistakes and sins, and this can be very painful.

---

14   Genesis 28:16,17
15   1 Peter 2:5

In pursuing God's call, you will have to make camp somewhere between the glorious house of God (Bethel), and the broken and defeated people of God. (Ai) If you focus only on Bethel, the glorious church of encounter, you are likely to have an exalted view of the church that can easily be shattered when you experience the brokenness and failures of God's people. However, if you focus only on the church that is defeated because of the brokenness and sin of its people, then you will become cynical and disillusioned.

I have known many people who have encountered the brokenness of church, and I have encountered it myself many times. I have experienced times when people in church hurt or disappointed me, and sometimes, I have been the one to hurt and disappoint others through my own weakness or sinfulness. Sometimes people walk away from the church or find a context that feels 'safer' to them. However, in doing this, they remove themselves from the context in which their call can be properly realised.

Pursuing the call of God will require you to make camp (like Abram) somewhere between these two realities, and to hold this tension as you, (like Abram) pursue the fulfilling of your call.

Negev—The Desert

The next place that Genesis twelve records that Abram travelled to was the Negev. The meaning of the Hebrew word Negev is dry, and accordingly, it is a desert. Along the journey of call there will be desert seasons. Certainly, David understood this. He was in one of those seasons when he penned the words of Psalm sixty-three,

"O God, you are my God, earnestly I seek you, my soul thirsts for you, my body longs for you, in a dry and weary land where there is no water."

It may come as a surprise, when on your journey with God's call, you experience these desert times. At such times, outwardly things do not seem to be happening and inwardly God seems to stand far from you. Perhaps this is why David, in his desert time, says of the Lord, "My soul thirsts for you." It wasn't just the outer thirst he was experiencing, but the inner thirst as well, a thirst for a sense of the presence of God.

There have been many times on my journey where it seems nothing is happening outwardly, and inwardly God seemed absent. These times though difficult, perform an important function. They cause your roots to grow deeper into God and they develop strength in your character. The call that God is placing on your life will require that you be well rooted in Him. Unless this happens, whatever is built on your life will be unstable and will not stand in trial. Jesus refers to this in His parable of the sower. In this parable, He talks about seed that fell on "rocky places where the soil was shallow[16]" and, when the sun of difficulty or persecution rose, it withered because it had no root.

The other aspect of this is that the desert seasons are sent to develop your character. This way, the call of God will have strong stems (character) to hang on. Paul wrote to the Christians in Rome,

"Suffering produces perseverance, perseverance character and character hope.[17]"

The hope of our calling is connected to developing a strong character that can consistently walk in that calling. To that end, God, in His wisdom, includes desert seasons on the journey of discovering and developing His call on your life. This way, through connection to Him, you will grow "fruit that will last[18]" and, by persevering through the desert times, you will develop the strength of character to carry that fruit.

Egypt – the land outside of call

The last place we will look at in Abram's journey is found in Genesis twelve verse ten,

16   Matthew 13:5
17   Romans 5:4
18   John 15:16

"Now there was a famine in the land, and Abram went down to Egypt to live there for a while because the famine was so severe."

In this time, Abram finds himself living outside of the call and the land of promise. We know from earlier in the chapter that Abram's call was to go to Canaan and ultimately that God would give to him and his descendants this land. Yet because of the famine he finds himself living outside of this call in the land of Egypt. Sometimes, in the journey of call, you will find yourself doing things, or in situations that seem to be outside of what resonates with you as the call of God on your life.

I remember a season when I was running an education centre, and out of frustration once praying "God, why am I doing this?" To which God almost casually replied "To feed your family." God used it to provide for my family, whilst I was also developing skills that would be used later in the outworking of God's call.

A Biblical example of this is found in the little book of Nehemiah in the Old Testament. In chapter one Nehemiah enquires about the Jewish remnant in Israel and how they are getting on. You can usually spot the passion of someone's heart by the questions they ask. Nehemiah's question is a strong clue that his heart and passion is connected to the community of Jewish exiles who returned to Jerusalem.

When he hears that the exiles are not doing well, his response again shows his heart. In Nehemiah chapter one verse four we read,

"When I heard these things, I sat down and wept. For some days I mourned and fasted and prayed before the God of Heaven."

Here, his passion is seen most clearly. Not only does the woeful report cause him to weep, but this goes on for days, prompting a period of fasting and prayer. Clearly the remnant community is strongly on his heart. In this, you see Nehemiah's call. However, at that time, Nehemiah was in the employment of King Artaxerxes as a cupbearer, living in the citadel of Susa, one of the capitals of the Persian Empire.

Obviously, both in his employment and his geographic location, he is a long way from where he feels his heart and call is.

As the story unfolds, you find that God grants Nehemiah favor with the king and Artaxerxes ends up releasing Nehemiah to do the work of rebuilding the walls of Jerusalem. The king provides not only letters of introduction so that Nehemiah can have safe passage to get there, but also timber to make beams for the gates of the walls. What Nehemiah discovered was that when he found himself in a place that felt like he was outside of his passion and the call of God, actually God had positioned him there to prepare him, and eventually resource the very work that was on his heart.

Like Nehemiah, some days you may find yourself heading to work thinking, "Why am I here? What am I achieving for God? Why am I serving a pagan king (or system) rather than my passion?" Likewise, Abram, could have asked, "Why am I forced to go into Egypt when I am called to possess Canaan?" For both Nehemiah, Abram, and you, these places can be where God brings forth preparation and provision which eventually will prepare, protect, and provide for, the call that God has on your life.

Conclusion

So, you see all these dynamics at work in Abram's life as he pursues the call that God gave him. Sometimes you may hold in your mind a utopian ideal of what it means to be a person of call, but the realities of the journey may gradually erode any utopian ideas you may have constructed. These realities include being a pilgrim with an unsure final destination; someone who lives in the tension of the polarity of the glorious and broken church; someone who experiences desert times of outward inactivity and inward aridity; and someone who experiences seasons where you find yourself working outside your passion and call.

Along the way, it is easy to become disillusioned, but it is easy to forget that to become disillusioned means losing our illusions. Our illusions around God's call are often connected to our ego, and the reality of the journey moves us from our ego need, into the truth of God's heart and call for us.

Understanding the contours of this journey can equip you to embrace each place as an important part of your journey of the outworking of God's call. Once you realise that the journey is shaped for the purpose of bringing forth the fulfilling of God's call, it is easier to embrace each step along the way.

But what if those steps are not just difficult, but catastrophic? What happens if you have a sense of prophetic destiny and everything in your life seems to take you away from that? How do you then relate to those prophecies? And how do you hold on to the hope that your gifts and talents will still be somehow used in the outworking of God's purposes? These are some of the questions we will be addressing as we look at call in the life of the biblical character Joseph.

JOSEPH

n Genesis thirty-seven, we first meet the young
Joseph, who verse two tells us was seventeen at
the beginning of the biblical account of his story.
We are not far into this account when we discover
that Joseph receives some dreams that he perceives
speak to him of God's call and his future.

In verse six he tells his brothers,

"Listen to this dream I had. We were binding
sheaves of corn out in the field when suddenly my
sheaf rose and stood upright, while your sheaves
gathered around mine and bowed down to it."

A second dream is recorded in verse nine. It reads,

"I had another dream, and this time the sun and
moon and eleven stars were bowing down to me."

At the age of seventeen, Joseph, through these
dreams, has a sense of destiny, and what he believes

to be God's call. Although he does not know the specifics of it, he understands that somehow it will involve him being raised up above his brothers, and even his father and mother. Like Joseph, some people at a fairly young age, have a sense of prophetic clarity about their future. Whether they receive it themselves (as in this case in a dream) or whether that is affirmed over their lives through prophetic words, they feel around them a sense of calling, or destiny, in a particular direction.

As it turns out, Joseph's dreams as a young man were surprisingly accurate, yet the things he received, although prophetic, did not constitute God's call on his life. What we find is that the function of prophecy is not to tell us our call, but to guide us towards it. Prophecy, whilst always future orientated, is intended to align you with God's current activity, which will move you towards a future reality.

In his first letter to the church in Corinth, the apostle Paul specifically wrote regarding the function of prophecy. He wrote,

"But everyone who prophesies speaks to man for their strengthening, encouragement and comfort.[1]

The Greek word for strengthening, refers to the act of building. Prophecy is meant to start something in your present that will build towards future significance. Joseph's prophetic dreams caused

---

1   1 Corinthians 14:3

him to speak out to his family what he had heard and seen. This then activates a series of events that, although he couldn't see it at the time, began to build towards the fulfillment of his call. In this way, prophecy operates in the now, in order to build towards the future.

The next word Paul uses is encouragement, which in the Greek means to call to one's side. Here prophecy calls us into alignment with God's wider purpose. Again, Joseph's dreams, and his confession of them begin to align his life with his call.

The final word Paul used is comfort. In the Greek this literally means "To speak closely." Prophetic words will carry an inner resonance that draws you towards them. They speak to your heart.

Just before we left for Canada, my wife and I visited a church in Dunedin. The pastor (who did not know me at all) there picked me out of the congregation and spoke the following word,

"God is repositioning and relocating you. There is a whole new season in God which is not about letting ancient path's go, but God is going to challenge your thinking and previous beliefs."

This word built my confidence in going and aligned me with what God was about to do. My study involved both connecting with the ancient paths of church history, but also challenging and previous thinking and beliefs. Needless to say, the word also resonated with my heart and inner desire.

In Joseph's case, what he did not yet realise was the great personal cost involved in the fulfilling of his call. Like Abram, the encounter puts him on the pilgrim's journey, meaning that he has to leave all that is familiar, and the community of his family, and head off to an undetermined and unknown future, carrying with him, only the dreams he received in his early years.

Joseph's dreams do not give him a road map to his call, this call is not discovered until much later. What he does receive, are words that activate and align him with that call.

Call and Catastrophe

At this point, Joseph encounters what can only be described as a series of catastrophic events. The first of these is the hatred, betrayal and violence of his brothers towards him. Ultimately, this leaves him battered and bruised and sent off to Egypt as a slave, while his brothers sell the lie to his father that he has been killed.

The loss of his family, the betrayal of his brothers, the loss of his freedom, and the impact on his subsequent life, to this seventeen-year-old boy is huge. In almost every way, Joseph suffers dislocation and trauma. People who have experienced this, in various ways, clearly struggle to survive such experiences, let alone connect them with God's call. In fact, understandably, there is a reluctance to even try to do so. People may respond by saying, "If this is God's call/purpose for me, then not only is God not a God of love but is possibly something a lot worse!" They may even forsake their faith entirely at this point.

I will never forget meeting a girl on a street outreach in Auckland city, who told me in no uncertain terms that if God did exist, then He was a bastard! She proceeded to tell me of the time when her father (who worked for the church) was away from their home, and a man broke in and raped her mother and attacked her. I then had no difficulty understanding why she had come to the conclusions she had.

The amazing thing is, that had she looked, she would have found people who in some way agreed with her, in the Bible. Ethan the Ezrahite who wrote Psalm eighty-nine is clearly writing out of this place of trauma and disillusionment. Having reviewed God's promises given to David in the first half of the psalm, where God says,

"I have sworn by My holiness—and I will not lie to David, that his line will continue forever, and his throne endure before me like the sun.[2]"

---

2   Psalm 89:35

He goes on to say in verse thirty-eight and thirty-nine,

"But you have rejected, you have spurned... you have renounced your covenant with your servant and defiled his crown in the dust."

Ethan lets God know, in no uncertain terms, that from his perspective, He has abandoned them, and has not been faithful to fulfill his covenant. Joseph, having received dreams of his promotion, could certainly have felt the same way, now that he has been attacked, and sold into slavery by his brothers. Trying to reconcile God's call from this dark place is extremely difficult.

Not only this, but later on Joseph is falsely accused of sexual assault and is cast into prison as a result. His dreams could have easily come back to mock him at this point, when faced with the stark reality of prison, the sting of injustice, and a sense of abandonment.

People who have encountered loss, abuse, injustice and disappointment on their journeys, are often left to live through the effects of this, wondering what it is all about. Some people have talked about God seeming silent at this time, with questions flung towards heaven going unanswered. C. S Lewis in his book, *A Grief Observed*, describes this experience. He wrote,

"After that, silence. You may as well turn away.

The longer you wait, the more emphatic the silence will become. There are no lights in the windows. It might be an empty house. Was it ever inhabited? It seemed so once. And that seeming was as strong as this. What can this mean? Why is He so present a commander in our time of prosperity and so very absent a help in time of trouble?[3]"

How in the midst of this can you possibly understand or connect with God's call?

Fitting these events into a puzzle that makes sense of them, may at various times in our lives be a luxury that is not afforded to us. Gerald Sittser in his book, *A Grace Disguised,* recounts his journey around the death of his wife, mother and young daughter in an accident caused by a drunk driver. He wrote,

"Suffering may be at its fiercest when it is random, for we are then stripped of even the cold comfort that comes when events, however cruel, occur for a reason.[4]"

It seems fairly certain that in the season of Joseph's life in which he encountered these catastrophes, he did not have a framework of meaning in which to understand the purpose of his experiences and connect them to God's call on his life.

---

3   C.S Lewis, A Grief Observed, Harper Collins e-books Loc 177
4   Gerald Sittser, A Grace Disguised, How the Soul Grows Through Loss, Zondervan, Michigan, 1995, 111

Gerald Sittser reflecting on his experience of trauma wrote,

"Loss may appear to be random, but that does not mean it is. It may fit into a scheme that surpasses even what our imaginations dare to think.[5]"

This was true in Joseph's case. Later in his life, it seems that Joseph is able to put the pieces of the puzzle together in a way that he understood and was able to connect them to God's call. Such is the advantage of retrospect, yet at many points along the way he was faced with the decision to trust God in the midst of painful and confusing realities.

The writer of Proverbs puts it this way,

"Trust in the Lord with all of your heart, and lean not on your own understanding, in all your ways acknowledge him, and he will direct your paths.[6]"

Interestingly, the writer exhorts us to trust the Lord with all of our heart, not with our head. The head may often not understand, but the heart can still choose to trust. Joseph's thoughts and process during those dark days are not recorded for us, but it does seem that somehow, in the midst of the pain of loss and injustice, Joseph's heart chose to hold onto faith, and believe in the One whose plan he could not see from where he stood. If you have stood in a similar place, you will face this choice as well.

---

5   Ibid., 120
6   Proverbs 3:5-6

Gifts and Call

At this juncture, let us pause to make an observation regarding how Joseph's gifts of leadership and prophetic insight interact with his call. For some, this can be an area of confusion. You may ask,

"Do my gifts constitute my call?"

"If I am gifted as a teacher, does that mean God has called me as a teacher?"

"If I have gifts of administration, am I then called as an administrator?"

As Joseph walks the pilgrim journey towards his call, you see in various ways and contexts his gifts being outworked. From an early age he carries a gift of prophetic insight, and this is seen again later in chapter forty when he interprets dreams for the cupbearer and baker in prison, and again in chapter forty-one where he interprets Pharaoh's dreams.

In like manner we see clearly that Joseph carries the gift of leadership. This is outworked in chapter thirty-nine in the house of Potiphar, where we read in verse six,

"So, he (Potiphar) left in Joseph's care everything he had; with Joseph in charge, he did not concern himself with anything."

Again, when Joseph is put in prison because he is falsely accused of sexually assaulting Potiphar's wife, we read,

"So, the warder put Joseph in charge of all those held in the prison, and he was responsible for all that was done there.[7]"

Finally, this leadership gift comes into play when Joseph is appointed by Pharaoh to his court. It says,

"So, Pharaoh said to Joseph, "I hereby put you in charge of the whole land of Egypt.[8]

The reason I point this out, is so that you understand that your gifts do not constitute your call. Although they will be used in the outworking of it, they do not constitute it. As we saw, Joseph's gifts of prophetic insight, leadership and administration were all used in the outworking of God's call, but they did not constitute the call itself.

This is a common confusion. I have sometimes heard people say, "I am gifted to lead; therefore, I am called to be a leader." Or "I am gifted to teach; therefore, I am called to be a teacher." Although your gifts will be use in the outworking of your call, they themselves are not your call. Your call provides the context in which your gifts will operate. God's call, links our gifts to a place, a people, or a specific purpose in God's heart for that time.

Also, sometimes you can be promoted on the basis of gifting, but there is still a journey of maturing needed to bring us into connection with God's call.

---

7   Genesis 39:32
8   Genesis 41:41

The promotion of Joseph in Potiphar's house on the basis of his gifting, did not connect with his ultimate call. However, it was part of God preparing Joseph for it. In my life I have experienced this, where I was brought into roles on the basis of gifting, and each time it has represented a time of growing and maturing, but not yet the fulfillment of God's call for me.

So, what then was the call on Joseph's life? We see it clearly stated in Genesis forty-five when Joseph finally reveals his identity to his brothers. Naturally enough, they are terrified on finding out that this powerful man is actually the brother they sold into slavery. In Joseph's response to them, we hear his life's call articulated. In Genesis forty-five verses five to seven Joseph says,

"And now, do not be distressed and do not be angry with yourselves for selling me here, because it was to save lives that God sent me ahead of you, for two years now there has been a famine in the land, and for the next five years there will be no ploughing or reaping. But God sent me ahead of you to preserve for you a remnant on the earth and to save your lives by a great deliverance."

All of Joseph's gifts, and his journey was so that the people of God would be saved through this time of famine, and not perish. Had they perished, God would not have been able to fulfill His promises to Abraham, and his plan for redemption of the world would have been derailed. God's call to Joseph was to go ahead and save the lives of his family, so that in the bigger picture, God's purposes could be fulfilled. This gives you two important insights about your call.

Firstly, it is not about you. As with Joseph, your call is always other focused. Call does not exist to help you feel successful, valuable or fulfilled, but exists to fulfill the purposes of God for the sake of others. My ego would wish this otherwise, yet like Joseph, the journey towards call meant a move from the starry-eyed dreamer of his youth, to a mature ruler, able to extend grace and love to his brothers, through the fulfilling of his call. In our very individualised and self-seeking world, it is important to make this distinction.

Secondly, in this instance, Joseph's call becomes apparent to him later in life. It becomes the lens by which he can look back over his life and understand what God was doing, and why. This is not always the case, but it can be. Therefore, you must remain open to the possibility that you might only understand your call and purpose in God, in retrospect, from the vantage point of history. Some even died in faith not receiving the things promised, but seeing them from distance[9], like Moses peering across to the promised land.[10]

---

9   Hebrews 11:13
10   Deuteronomy 32

I believe they knew they fulfilled God's call, but also knew they were part of a bigger picture, yet to be revealed.

Looking back on the journey

As we have journeyed with Joseph and God's call on his life, we have observed how his dreams operated to align him to God's call but did not operate as a road map to his call. In this, you may get a better picture of the function of the prophetic on your journey with God's call, that it works in the now, to orientate you to the fulfilling of that call.

Also, we learned that Joseph's gifts did not constitute his call, but we saw how they were used in the fulfilling of that call. Understanding this, may prevent you from making the mistake of thinking your gifts constitute your call. Instead, call provides the context, in which our gifts are used. Also, promotion on the basis of gifts, may only constitute steps towards a call, which God uses to mature and develop you.

Finally, like Abraham, Joseph found his call taking him away from the comforts of his home and putting him on a pilgrim's journey. On the way, he faces catastrophic events which caused him great suffering. Faced with these, Joseph had a choice to trust God in the face of suffering, believing that these things had not invalidated his call, but, in a way that he could not have understood at the time, would actually be part of it.

In like manner, you too may have faced losses, rejection, injustice and failure. Like Joseph, you may have to hold on to the belief that although you see no good in these experiences, God has not abandoned you, and that these experiences do not invalidate your call, and may even connect with His call and purpose on your life in ways that are not initially apparent to you.

The narrative of Genesis, captures much of Joseph's outer journey, but what about his inner journey? Along the way, Joseph would have walked a deep interior process, involving him coming to understand himself, and learning how to authentically walk the path towards the realisation of God's call.

On the journey of discovering God's call on your life, you also will face questions like, "What is my authentic self?" "What do I really want?" and perhaps, "What are some of the things that are preventing me from aligning my life with these truths?" In our next chapter, we connect with the New Testament character Martha, as she faces these same questions.

MARTHA

"Noverim me, noverim me."
("May I know You, may I know myself.")

St Augustine

The journey towards our true selves

In the New Testament, we meet the character of Martha in various places. It appears that she was the sister of Lazarus (whom Jesus raised from the dead), as recorded in John chapter eleven, and also the older sister of Mary. In Luke chapter ten, there is a well-known account of a time when Jesus visited the village where Martha and Mary lived. Verse thirty-eight says that Martha opened her home to Jesus (and presumably His disciples as well.)

Verses thirty-nine to forty-one records an incident that happened in her home. It reads,

"She (Martha) had a sister called Mary, who sat at the Lord's feet listening to what He said. But Martha was distracted by all the preparations that had to be made. She came to Him and asked 'Lord, don't You care that my sister has left me to do all the work by myself? Tell her to help me!'

'Martha, Martha,' the Lord answered, you are worried and upset about many things, but only one thing is needed. Mary has chosen what is better, and it will not be taken away from her.'"

Over the years, people many have felt that Jesus was a bit unfair to Martha, who just wanted some help preparing the lunch! However, a closer look may reveal some interesting aspects to Jesus' response to her.

Firstly, verse thirty-eight tells us that it was Martha's initiative to invite and host Jesus into her home. Although we don't know her motivation for sure, it is likely her motivation in some way involved wanting to be with Jesus. However, when Jesus arrived at her house, she was not actually being with Him because she was "distracted by all the preparations". What was worse, her sister Mary was sitting calmly at Jesus' feet, doing the very thing that she wanted to do but felt she couldn't. I think it is likely that this, as much as her need for help in the kitchen, caused her anger to burn against Mary and precipitated her angry outburst at Jesus.

It is good to examine for a moment why Martha did not feel free to do what her heart desired to do. I think her reasons would fall into two categories: social (external) and personal (internal). Socially, there were expectations on hosts. The honour of her house and the cultural expectation of hospitality was on her shoulders. Also, as older sister, she may have been used to being the responsible one, looking after the younger, less responsible, siblings.

Secondly, there may have been other personal reasons. Martha perhaps had inward motivations around wanting to be seen as capable and successful. This is a natural desire, if I am honest, and one that is deeply imbedded in my life. There have been times, when I faced the humbling truth that my desire to serve Jesus, actually was rooted in the desire to be seen as capable and successful. Even worse, this stemmed from a subtle (and maybe not so subtle) sense of pride. Part of Martha's motivation in inviting Jesus to her home may have been that others would see this and know that Jesus (the popular Rabbi) chose to dine with her. This is spirituality on display. Here we gain our personal sense of worth and pride from the public perception of our connection to Jesus. Thus, Martha's actions reflect a mixture of cultural expectations and interior motivations. I think all of us can relate to, in some way, the pressure of culture to fulfil its expectations and demands. The possibility of shame or social disapproval is a powerful factor in shaping our lives. Likewise, our inner sense of self and the need to feel successful and admired also often lie in the substrata of our motivations, even in the process of serving Jesus.

Encountering Jesus

All these things lay under the surface until, under the pressure of the circumstances, Martha's anger manifests into the room so that now it has to be dealt with. Similarly, you can go along for quite a time (maybe years) doing what is expected of you and feeding your inner need for approval by being the person you want other people to see and like. Then suddenly, in a given situation, you crack, and your anger testifies to the fact that you actually are not happy. At such times, like Martha, you can even turn to Jesus and exclaim,

"Lord, don't you care.[1]"

"Don't you care that I am unhappy?"

"Don't you care that I am working my butt off

---

1   John 11:40

here, sacrificing, while others sit round?"

"Don't you care about me, about what I want?"

At this point, Jesus does two things. The first thing he does is he calls Martha's name, twice. This is significant. The first time, it is just to get her attention and to help her break out of the storm of her emotions. Unless you break with these things, the only thing getting your attention will be the feelings and emotions of that moment. In this place you will only see how unfair it is, and how bad, or how irresponsible others are.

Not only this, but you can even 'rehearse' these emotions over years. I have to confess that I have been guilty of doing this at times. The effect of this is that those feelings extend their influence over your life, over an extended period of time. As you re-experience and rehearse that event or situation, these emotions imprint onto your soul. The problem is that while these emotions rage, you feel increasingly justified in your hurt and anger, and increasingly deaf to any other perspective.

But then, Jesus calls her name a second time. This time it is to draw her eyes to look away from herself and to look at Him, because He has something to say. Jesus calls Martha to look at Him, into His eyes.

There is a great scripture in Psalm thirty-two verse eight which reads,

"I will instruct you and teach you in the way you should go. I will guide you with my eye."

Jesus gets Martha to look into His eyes so that He can guide her with His heart. Once He has her looking at Him, Jesus brings a word of knowledge that describes the state of her soul. He says,

"You are worried and upset about many things.[2]"

Jesus uses two Greek words here. The first is *merimna*, which means to be drawn in different directions. The second word, *thorubazo*, means troubled. So together we could say she was troubled or disturbed because she was conflicted, drawn in two different directions. As we noted earlier, Martha wanted to sit at Jesus' feet, like Mary, but she didn't feel free to follow what she really wanted to do.

Jesus' words expose the state of Martha's heart and Martha, perhaps for the first time, gets to see it. Jesus' words bring to light Martha's false self. This is the self that is busy fulfilling everyone else's expectations and conforming to the culture, projecting her ideal self, the way she wants to be seen to the world, but is not true to itself. This is the self that is busy doing the expected role, being the good host, being the responsible big sister, but inwardly burns and is increasingly tired of carrying that role. She also is increasingly aware, and resents, that she is not free to do what she really wants to do. This false

---

2   John 11:41

self is also rooted in pride and gratifying her need to see herself as successful, busy, and in demand. Yet all the time, like Martha, this false self is binding us up and taking us away from our true selves.

I believe, it is this true self that Jesus is talking about in Matthew sixteen verse thirty-six when He says,

"What good will it be for a man if he gains the whole world, yet forfeits his soul? Or what can a man give in exchange for his soul?"

Too many of us exchange our true selves for other things. We may gain many things, fulfil many roles, achieve much, but have forfeited our true selves in the process. Jesus asks, if we forfeit ourselves, what good have we then gained?

The journey towards knowing and fulfilling your call will involve moving away from your false self and embracing your true self. This journey is able to happen when, in a moment of crises, or as a spiritual discipline, you look into Jesus' eyes and allow Him to reflect your false selves back to you, just as Jesus did to Martha in this instance. Such encounters can be difficult and disarming, but Jesus's intent is to set you free. You will never be free to discover and do what your heart desires, unless you allow Jesus to take you to this place.

As mentioned, this can happen in a moment of crises (like Martha) when a crack in your successful persona appears and you let slip the reality of your heart, or, by developing the practice of meditation which enables you to look into Jesus' eyes, and allow Him to reflect you back to yourself. This practice involves taking time to be quiet (silence), to be alone (solitude), and to give your attention to Jesus. This is not just a one-off event, but a practice by which you connect your lives with the gaze of God. There God will increasingly reveal to you your false self (the one built on your insecurities, aspirations, and the expectations of others) and will bring to you the revelation of who you truly are in Him. The famous sixteenth century mystic Teresa de Avila in her classic book, *The Interior Castle,* wrote, "As I see it, we shall never succeed in knowing ourselves unless we seek to know God."[3] Your journey with God, will, if you allow it, bring you to self-discovery.

In my journey, my ability to know, and be comfortable with who I am, and who I am not, has grown out of seeing myself reflected back to me, in eyes of God. In Matthew sixteen after Peter reveals that he has received revelation about the true identity of Jesus, Jesus turns to him in verse eighteen, and reflects Peter back to himself. He says,

"And I tell you that you are Peter, and on this rock, I will build my church."

---

3   Avila, Teresa of, Interior Castle. Translated and Edited by E. Allison Peers. Page 38

In the revelation of Jesus, you will also, like Peter, find the revelation of your true self and God's call and purpose for you. Usually, God's call will resonate at a deep level with your true self. The journey towards knowing and fulfilling God's call will involve getting free from the false self and coming into harmony with who God created you to be.

The impact of this encounter on Martha is perhaps seen later in John chapter eleven, which records the death and raising of Lazarus, the brother of Martha and Mary. In this narrative you see a switching of roles. This time it is Martha who rushes to see Jesus, while Mary stays away, back at the house. I may be reading too much into this, but it seems that Martha now has a greater freedom to be where she wants to be, and it is from this place that she encounters Jesus' resurrection power, which brings about a great release of God's Kingdom on earth. John chapter eleven verse forty-five tells us that, as a result, many believed in Jesus.

Imagine the impact on the world when you get free to embrace your true self and get free from all the things that hold you back and keep you hiding in a false persona. I am not advocating self-emancipation, it is important to allow Jesus to lead this process, to discover your true self in connection with Him. But when it happens, the result is life giving, even if the process can be a bit messy.

Looking back on the journey

By looking deeper at what is happening in Martha's encounter with Jesus, you have glimpsed an important dynamic of the journey towards God's call. You will have seen that the journey is not only outward but also involves an inner journey. It is here that you encounter Jesus and are enabled to see your false self, and let Jesus lead you to freedom. Only then can you see clearly what it is you truly want, and this frequently aligns with your call.

Walking this journey will involve embracing times of contemplation, silence, and solitude. Here, you look into God's face and allow Him to guide you with His eye. Without this, the noise and demands of both the inner and outer world will prevent you from ever engaging with the process of inner formation needed to understand your true self, and consequently God's call.

Like Martha, this process can be precipitated by the relationships and experiences you encounter in the day-to-day living of life. Mary's presence and her choices became the spark that ignited Martha's encounter with Jesus. Martha's angry response toward her is typical of our response when we meet people who require something from us that we aren't willing to give. Yet, as we saw in Martha's case, it was this very thing that led her to encounter Jesus and, through that encounter, to be changed and enabled to step forth into her true self and call.

In the next chapter, we will examine this dynamic further by looking at the call and ministry of the apostle Paul.

THE APOSTLE PAUL

Mother Teresa of Calcutta

Acts chapter nine records the dramatic account of the conversion of Saul the Pharisee, later to become known as Paul the apostle. Immediately after Saul's encounter, Ananias is sent to Saul who prays for him to restore his sight. In God's word to Ananias, we catch a glimpse of the call that God has on Saul's life.

Verse fifteen reads,

"But the Lord said to Ananias, "Go! This man is my chosen instrument to carry My Name before the

Gentiles and their kings, and before the people of Israel. I will show him how much he must suffer for my name."

Acts thirteen records how, many years later, Saul (now named Paul) and his companion Barnabas were commissioned by the church in Antioch to their first missionary journey, which would involve them preaching the gospel of Jesus to both Jews and Gentiles. As they went, they established groups of new believers in many cities. However, the aspect of Paul's call that I want to focus on is found in God's final sentence to Ananias, "I will show him how much he must suffer for my name".

I have to confess, that I do not often want to connect God's call on my life with the experience of suffering. More often, I think of walking in God's call in terms of having experiences that are life affirming and life giving. I picture my gifts being used to change nations as I walk in and impart the blessing of God to others. The idea of ongoing or even occasional suffering clearly seems at odds with this picture. Even more disturbing is the possibility that suffering could actually be an integral part of that picture.

Before I embark further down this path, I feel I need to say that in no way do I wish to minimise or trivialise the difficulties associated with human suffering. Nor do I want to paint a happy face on it, or imply that by attaching meaning to suffering we can sanctify it, or obscure the true difficulties of walking that path. I have journeyed with too many people who have encountered genuine suffering to dishonour them by doing that. I offer my thoughts more as one who speaks from the outside of suffering, rather than from the inside, and I recognise there is a vast difference between these two places.

My hope in writing this chapter is firstly that those who suffer would know that the presence of suffering in their lives far from invalidating God's call, may actually be part of that call, as it was for Paul. Secondly to alert us to the ways that the presence of those who suffer amongst us, carry a special part in the purpose and call of God.

So, what did God mean when He said to the newly converted Saul, "I will show him how much he must suffer for my name"? In the Bible, names carry specific significance. The *NIV Dictionary of the Bible* says,

"The name, moreover, was the person as he has been revealed; for example, the "name of the Lord" signified the Lord in the attributes he had manifested.[1]"

Thus, Paul's call to suffer for God's name connected his suffering with the manifestation of the

---

1   The New International Dictionary of the Bible. Editors J.D Douglas and Merrill C. Tenney, Zondervan, Grand Rapids MI, U.S.A, 690

character and the presence of God. How does this work? In John chapter nine, Jesus and his disciples come across a man born blind and the disciples ask Jesus a question that clearly shows their worldview. They ask,

"Rabbi, who sinned, this man or his parents, that he was born blind?[2]"

In their view, sickness or suffering was the result of sin. To them, that was such a self-evident truth that they skipped straight to the question of who was to blame? Their hidden logic was that sin causes sickness and, if someone is sick, then somebody sinned. The only question was: was it him or his parents?

Since he was born blind, one wonders how he could have sinned before he was born to deserve this affliction? However, the disciple's belief was so ingrained, that this logical anomaly didn't even occur to them. The idea that sin causes sickness runs deep and, deep down, our hearts can quietly go about the task of apportioning blame. Somewhere, somehow.

However, Jesus' answer blows their worldview apart. In verse three He says,

"Neither this man nor his parents sinned..."

Suddenly, the disciples are thrown into a different universe. If suffering cannot be tied down to a specific cause (namely sin) then how could they

---

2   John 9:1

understand it? More importantly how could they avoid it? In this new world Jesus just created, their conception of cause and effect regarding suffering is now blown apart and replaced with a chaotic void of confusion and uncertainty.

Into the ruins of this previous view of suffering, Jesus inserts a whole new paradigm. He says,

"...but this happened that the work of God might be displayed in his life.[3]"

This is radical. It appears that the 'this' in Jesus' statement refers to the man's blindness, and the word He uses for displayed (or manifest) is the Greek word *phaneros*, which means 'open to sight'. It seems Jesus is saying that this man's lack of sight means that the work of God has become open to sight.

This is an entirely new paradigm for the disciples. Previously sickness or disease was the result of sin and someone was responsible. But Jesus seems to be saying that the glory of God can be made manifest, or brought to sight, through someone's sickness or suffering and God's Name or character may also be made manifest.

Most people who know the rest of the story would argue that God's glory is seen when Jesus heals this man, yet this conversation happened before the healing, and Jesus heals him in an unusual

---

3   John 9:3

way. John nine verse six records that Jesus spat on the ground, made mud with his saliva, and put it on the man's eyes. Then he sends him to wash in the pool of Siloam (and John notes that Siloam means 'sent').

This is interesting, as the word apostle (*apostolos* in Greek) also means 'to send' or 'sent'. So here Jesus anoints this blind man with his saliva (and mud) and he is sent (made an apostle) while he is still blind to obey what Jesus tells him to do. Is it possible that Jesus anoints the afflicted and sends them (like an apostle) to us to display His character and glory?

I expect you to then ask,

"How can suffering and affliction display God's glory?"

"How can blindness, autism, or cancer display God's glory?"

It seems blasphemous, even perverted, to suggest that mental illness or physical sickness could in any way bring glory to God.

One way of perhaps approaching this is to understand the gift that those in pain bring to us. In Jesus' parable about loving our neighbour, the Samaritan is revealed as good only in the presence of the suffering and beaten man. Likewise, the Pharisee and Levite's character are judged by their response, or lack of it, to the suffering man. One way or another, the presence of the suffering individual brings to light what is in our hearts. In this way, the work of God is made manifest.

If this is true, then is it possible that the person carrying the affliction can actually be fulfilling the call of God by being 'sent' by God (as an apostle) to make manifest His work in the life of those around him or her.

We easily forget, that when God wanted to manifest Himself to the world, He sent Jesus to dwell among us as One who served and suffered. One prophetic description of Jesus is a passage that many people with sicknesses and disabilities might unfortunately relate to. It reads,

"He had no beauty or majesty to attract us to Him, nothing in His appearance that we should desire Him. He was despised and rejected by men, a man of sorrows, familiar with suffering. Like one from whom men hide their faces...[4]"

On top of the pain of disability or sickness, many also feel the pain of rejection, of not being attractive or desirable to others, even of people withdrawing from them because of their condition. Isaiah prophesies that God would be among us in this guise.

Matthew twenty-five records the parable of the sheep and goats. Jesus calls our attention to the mystery of His presence in the suffering and vul-

---

4   Isaiah 53:2-3

nerable among us when He says to the ones who cared for those who were hungry, naked, sick, or imprisoned,

"Whatever you did for one of the least of these brothers of mine, you did for Me.[5]"

When you journey with those who are suffering, the understanding that they could be Christ in your midst, sent to manifest the state of your heart, is a powerful thought. In Paul's letter to the Galatians, we discover that he met them when he was experiencing sickness. He wrote

"As you know, it was because of an illness that I first preached to you the gospel.[6]"

Yet apparently, the Galatians responded to him with great openness. He continues,

"And even though my illness was a trial to you, you did not treat me with contempt or scorn. Instead, you welcomed me as if I were an angel of God, as if I were Christ Jesus Himself.[7]"

Wow! If you, like the Galatians, could receive those suffering, as an 'angel of God', or even as "Christ Jesus Himself", then you would be open to receive the good news through them. This requires that you see the sick or suffering one as an apostle (one who is sent) to minster to you, so that through them the work of salvation can come.

---

5   Matthew 25:40
6   Galatians 4:13
7   Galatians 4:14

I have experienced some of this myself. Some years back, I had a season of working with handicapped people as a chaplain to their group homes. What I soon realised was that it was they, who drew out the work of God in me, so that I could enter more fully into His salvation. Consistently, it was I, not them, who walked away most blessed. Many of these folks, as well as others with mental illness attended the church that I pastored. I always chose to see their presence among us as a gift that helped us keep real in our faith and challenged us to expand our hearts. In this way, we were saved from religious hype, or being too impressed with our abilities, and enabled somehow to become more loving, more authentic, more Christ-like.

Paul, however, also speaks a message to those who suffer. In his writing, he showed that he understood the mysterious connection between the power of God and suffering. More specifically, he understood how this is bound together in the person of Christ. Because of this, he made it the central prayer of his life. He wrote,

"I want to know Christ, the power of His resurrection and the fellowship of sharing in his suffering.[8]"

The Greek word for fellowship is *koinonia*, which essentially means 'to have in common'. When we look at Paul's life, his imprisonments, floggings,

---

8   Philippians 3:10

and rejection, it does seem that Christ's sufferings overflowed into his life. But in his second letter to the Corinthians, Paul reveals that he has a personal painful ongoing condition that he calls the 'thorn in his flesh.' Like any painful or debilitating condition, Paul begs God to take it away from Him. In verse eight he wrote,

"Three times I pleaded with the Lord to take it away from me.[9]"

Those with painful conditions may have often visited this place, probably more than three times. Even Jesus, when facing the cross, prayed,

"My Father, if it is possible, may this cup be taken from me.[10]"

Yet somehow, Paul found that God's grace met him in this place. He records God saying to him,

"My grace is sufficient for you, for my power is made perfect in weakness.[11]"

This is a mystery. One I almost dare not speak to. The inexpressible grace given to the one who shares in the ministry of suffering. I have seen it in others, and I pray that I will experience it at the time I may be called to undergo suffering. God says, His power is made perfect (mature) in suffering. The problem is that suffering doesn't look powerful, it looks like Jesus on the cross, in excruciating pain, powerless,

---

9   2 Corinthians 12:8
10   Matthew 26:39
11   2 Corinthians 12:9

naked, mocked, and apparently defeated. Yet at that very moment, on the cross, God was at work bringing salvation to the earth and defeat to the devil.

Conclusion

So, we have seen that God's call can include the call to suffer. Paul's call to suffer for God's Name meant that through his suffering, the character and power of God would be revealed. If you understand suffering this way, then you will not make the same mistake as the disciples and see suffering always as a result of sin. Instead, you will understand that God may be sending the suffering person to you as an apostle to bring forth or make manifest the work of His salvation in your life. And, if you are the one who suffers, you may understand that God has sent you as an apostle to achieve His work in the lives of those around you.

If you understand this dynamic, then you can honour those among you who carry this call. Receiving them (like the Galatians to Paul) as angels of God, even as Christ Himself. In this way God's salvation, and His hidden power, can come to You. In relationship to them you are saved from your own selfishness, from your pride, and from your own addiction to comfort and power.

Paul's life certainly fulfilled God's call as he walked his journey of faith. In walking your journey, you might ask,

"Are there signposts that can help me on this journey?" Or,

"Are there seasons connected to the development and out working of God's call, and if so, how do I discern and navigate these seasons?"

Some of us may have walked through seasons of life and ministry and looked back with questions about its effectiveness and even with a degree of pain about what was or wasn't achieved. The next chapter looks at the life of John the Baptist and examines how his journey with call speaks to some of these questions.

JOHN THE BAPTIST

The story of John the Baptist's call begins before his conception, with an angelic visitation to his father, where John's name and mission are clearly revealed to his father. In Luke one, verse seventeen, the angel said to Zechariah,

"And he will go before the Lord, in the spirit and power of Elijah... to make ready a people prepared for the Lord."

This being the case, the circumstances of John's birth, his call, and the Nazarite vow attached to him, would have shaped John's life right from the start.

Decades later, when John's ministry is in full swing, the priests and Levites demanded that he give account of himself, saying, "Who are you?[1]"

---

1   John 1:22

His answer, echoed the call given to his father, drawing from the words of the prophet Isaiah,

"I am the voice of one calling in the desert. Make straight the way for the Lord.[2]"

It is evident that for John, his life's call was connected with, and was expressed through this significant Scripture. When pressed to articulate his call, it was these words that he returned to.

John would have known all the Scriptures, but these particular verses carried special significance and life for him. He would have known the words of Deuteronomy eight verse three, later quoted by Jesus which says,

"Man does not live by bread alone, but on every word that comes from the mouth of God." Two words stand out here. The first is the word 'live,' which takes its root from the Greek word *zoe*, which the Vines Expository Dictionary defines as, "life in its absolute sense[3]".

The second is the word 'word,' which in the Greek is *rhema*. Again, Vines defines this as, "That which is spoken," or, "individual Scriptures which the Spirit brings to us.[4]"

Therefore, if we are to live this *zoe* life, life in its fullest sense, which Jesus said that He came to give

---

2   John 1:23, Isaiah 40:3

3   Vines Complete Expository Dictionary of Old and New Testament Words. Thomas Nelson Publishers, Nashville Tennessee, 368

4   Ibid., 683

us,[5] then we must live out of the words that the Spirit breathes life on, which connect with who we are, and what God has for us to do.

For me, such a Scripture is in First Chronicles twenty-eight verse ten which records David's commission to Solomon. It reads,

"Consider now, for the Lord has chosen you to build a temple as a sanctuary. Be strong and do the work."

This was one of those 'God-breathed' Scriptures for me. In it, I understood that my call was to co-work with God to build His church, using the gifts and resources that I have been given.

Throughout my life, in various seasons and places, I have sought to be obedient to this call.

Isaiah forty, would have been a beacon and guiding Scripture to John throughout his life. When everyone else was confused about who John was, and what he was doing, these verses gave him a context of meaning in which to understand his life and call.

Not only did these Scriptures give John a platform to stand on, as the details of his call came together, it also gave him the ability to recognise and discern the seasons of that call. Before I look at this aspect of John's call, let me first say that I understand that life seldom falls into neat categories. Having said this, it is still helpful to identify three

---

5   John 10:10

general seasons visible on John's life. These are the seasons of preparation, operation and withdrawal. These seasons do not operate as distinct, sequential seasons, but rather as strands woven throughout our lives. In this way, you are perpetually preparing, operating and ending in different ways. Sometimes letting go of one thing is in itself preparation for the release of a new operation of God's grace.

Let us now examine the characteristics of each of these seasons.

Preparation

Preparation is linked to developing towards a specific task, for instance you may prepare for an exam, or to go on a camping trip. This requires specific activities that find their fulfilment in doing that for which you prepared.

If we go back to Ephesians two verse ten which says that, "We are God's workmanship," then we recognise that His hand is already at work, shaping and preparing us for the works that He has prepared for us to do. This involves your place, your background and your life experiences.

For John, part of his call was to be 'a voice crying in the desert'[6] and this required that he dwell literally in the desert. In Matthew three we read,

---

6   John 1:23

"In those days John the Baptist came preaching in the desert of Judea... John's clothes were made of camel hair, and he had a leather belt around his waist. His food was locusts and wild honey."[7]

John's location was linked to his vocation. This may differ for different people, for example, Paul was called to a people group (the Gentiles) which required that he travel to various places.

Sometimes, (like Abraham and Joseph) God may require that you shift from where you are to fit your call, but equally, God may have placed you in a certain place or position from which his call can be out-worked. I think a great example of this in the Bible is Joanna. Joanna is not a well-known character, but her call was vital in enabling Jesus' ministry to function. Joanna was the wife of a man named Chuza, who was the manager of Herod's household. This position would have held great responsibility and would have been well remunerated, thus Chuza and Suzanna would have been well off. In Luke chapter eight we read that Joanna, and other woman, were helping to financially support Jesus' ministry out of their own means.

Whilst John was called to prepare the way for Jesus, Joanna was called to support Jesus' ministry financially. In order to fulfil his call, John had to live in a desert. In order for Joanna to fulfil her call,

---

7   Matthew 3:1, 3

she and her husband had to live in a grand house (perhaps connected to Herod's) and have a good income.

You can trust that God is working throughout your life to prepare you to fulfil the unique works that he has prepared for you to do. It is faith that enables you to believe that He is doing this work, and to submit into His hand as He prepares and positions you for this call.

You might ask, "if God is doing this work, do I have any part to play in it?" Here we encounter a paradox in that it is God's work, but we too are called to work. Paul expresses this paradox in Philippians two verses twelve to thirteen when he wrote,

"... continue to work out your salvation with fear and trembling—for it is God who works in you to will and to act according to His good purpose."

Both are needed. This is seen in the Old Testament character of Samson. His parents, like John, received his call before he was born. He, like John, was also called to embrace a Nazarite vow. However, as his story unfolds, you see that Samson's character shows that he had not done the work needed to walk faithfully in his call. The result was that he suffered loss and defeat. This was not God's desire for his life.

Operation

For both John and Joanna, there was a time when preparation turned into operation. In this time, the previous shaping and positioning of their lives, comes into line with God's call. In Greek, there are two words for time, *Chronos* and *Kairos*. Chronos is the ongoing advance of time, like the ticking of the clock, whereas Kairos refers to time marked by specific characteristics. Kairos time is where preparation meets operation. This is where the preparation and positioning of your life, connect with the purpose and call of God.

We see this with Joseph, when his brothers come seeking food and bow before him, as he had seen in his dream as a teenager. In this moment, Joseph sees how the experiences and preparation of his life, intersect with the purpose and call of God. Suddenly, he realises that all that had happened to him in his life to this point, had been so that he could provide for, and protect his family; and in doing this protect God's chosen and covenanted people and His ongoing purposes.

Withdrawing

Because John knew his call, he also knew when he had completed his part, and could withdraw. Like someone running a relay race, he knew his part, and was able to pass on the baton gracefully. This can be difficult for some people if their call and identity are too closely linked. If you draw your identity and significance from your call, then you will find it difficult to hand it over when the time comes. Conversely, if you are secure in who you are as a son or daughter of God, then you have freedom to step into God's call, and away from it, when the time comes because you won't fear losing who you are or eroding your sense of self-worth. John displays this sense of security when he said,

"He must become greater, and I must become less[8]".

Disillusionment

Before we leave looking at John, there is one more aspect of his journey which I think may be helpful. Matthew eleven records John sitting in prison full of doubts and questions. Looking back, he now wonders whether he has got it all wrong, and asks Jesus,

"Are you the one who was to come, or should we expect another?[9]"

John, having received his call, having walked in it, and then successfully discerning its operation and seasons, is still found at the end of his life, lost

8   John 3:30
9   Luke 7:19

in this place of disillusionment.

I recall walking with a friend and hearing his struggles and doubts around his call. He seemed to be saying "I have done my best to know and walk in my call, and yet as I look back, I'm still confused, unsure whether I achieved God's call, or achieved anything that seems to fit with what I had hoped to see."

Within this experience can even be a sense of disappointment with Jesus, it seems that to some degree this was how John the Baptist felt. As with John, Jesus may seem to have not done what you expected Him to do. He may not have fitted the mold of your expectations. At this point, there may be even a temptation to even step back from your faith as you struggle with this disparity. I think we can take heart that John the Baptist faced exactly these same questions, and from this place, He sent out a distress call to Jesus.

It appears that a large part of John's confusion and questions came from the fact that Jesus' ministry did not fit with the picture that he had believed, and had preached, to the people. Jesus had not ushered in the expected physical Kingdom of God, nor had He rained judgement on the enemies of Israel and all the unrighteous. John looked in vain for the 'baptism of fire[10] that he had prophesied that would uproot every unfruitful tree[11], and thresh the wheat

10   Luke 3:16
11   Luke 3:9

and burn up its chaff in an unquenchable fire.[12] Things had not played out according to his expectations.

In a modern context, the equivalent might be that the church did not grow, revival tarried, you saw few baptisms, evil, immorality and addictions continued unabated, you were not in demand as a preacher, family members remained closed to the gospel, projects started with great passion and promise, did not end in like glory.

If I am honest, I have faced these experiences and disillusionments myself. Many things that I have passionately poured my life into, did not seemingly bear great fruit, and one is left wondering, "Is this it?"

John asked this question as he sat in jail, the prisoner of the unrighteous Herod, knowing that Herod continued his evil and immoral rule without any seeming judgement or action from God, while John, with death potentially imminent, is struggling not to give himself up to disillusionment and despair. John would perhaps identify with the words of the psalmist,

"This is what the wicked are like—always carefree, they increase in wealth. Surely in vain I have kept my heart pure, in vain I have washed my hands in innocence... When I tried to understand all this, it was oppressive to me.[13]"

12   Luke 3:17
13   Psalm 73:12,13, 16

Jesus' response to him, in this dark place is helpful to those of us who have grappled with these issues. Firstly, he directs John's attention to what has happened, and away from what has not happened. Jesus says,

"Go back to John and report to him what you hear and see. The blind receive sight, the lame walk, those who have leprosy are cured, the deaf hear, the dead are raised, and the good news preached to the poor.[14]"

Often, from this place, it is easy to get overwhelmed with what did not happen. You think of the people who weren't helped, the ongoing prevalence of unrighteousness, the programmes that failed, or the things that were initially stirred to action, but died down again. From here, you forget the things that did happen. The grace that was released, those who were helped, and those who experienced and heard good news. Jesus gently turns John's eyes back, to look again at the good things that have happened. Secondly, He says to John,

"Blessed is the man who does not fall away on account of me.[15]"

The Greek word translated here as, 'does not fall away', is *skandalisthe*, which takes its root from the word *skandalon*, meaning to be offended. Vines tells us that this word refers to the part of a trap where

14   Matthew 11:4
15   Matthew 11:6

the bait is attached[16]. The Greek word for blessing used here is *markarizo* which can also be translated as, happy. So, Jesus is saying to John, that if he took the bait of offence because things didn't look like he expected, he would have forfeited his happiness. If John had done this, he would have died bitter and disillusioned. Hopefully, he heeded Jesus' warning, and was able to take joy in what he did see, and trust God for the rest.

Sometimes, like John, you may find yourself drawn by the bait of being offended by unmet expectations. At that time, heeding Jesus' word to John can also lead you away from disillusionment, and towards a better place. It is also good to note that encountering disillusionment and disappointment on the road to pursuing God's call does not mean that you did not fulfil God's call. John definitely had fulfilled God's call, but he still visited this place.

In Isaiah fifty-five verse eight God says,

"For My thoughts are not your thoughts, neither are your ways My ways."

God is often operating at quite a different level than us, so that your thoughts and expectations may not be met, or met in ways that you don't fully understand. This has to be understood and accepted if you are not to forfeit the happiness (blessing) that

---

16   Vines Complete Expository Dictionary of Old and New Testament Words. Thomas Nelson Publishers, Nashville Tennessee, 441

comes with co-working with God in the outworking of your call.

Conclusion

From the perspective of history, it is clear to us how John's call fitted in the wider purposes of God. This would not have been so clear to John, certainly not towards the end of his life.

Jesus's words were intended to help John finish well, even though he did not have all of the answers. Your call will also fit into the wider kaleidoscope of God's redemptive plan for humanity. You won't see it all, but abundant joy and meaning can be found in doing your part so that collectively the manifest wisdom of God will be made known.[17]

The apostle Paul knew this joy. At the end of his life, he wrote,

"I have fought the good fight; I have finished the race[18]."

I believe that we too can know the joy of running our race and doing the works that He gave for us to do.

For John the strands of preparation, operation and withdrawal wove through his life. I too, see these strands woven through my life as I walk my journey with God. Every end is a beginning, prepa-

17   Ephesians 3:10
18   2 Timothy 4:7

ration co-exists with operation, and between the ongoing function of these, I also see the grace of transition. This is where God, who does all things well, prepares me for leaving, or for the operation of next thing that is coming. John's ministry itself is a testimony to the wisdom of God who sends grace to "prepare the way of the Lord.[19]"

Understanding the existence and characteristics of these seasons, may provide you with a lens through which you can better discern the activity of God on your life, constantly preparing, operating and ending in various ways.

Lastly, for those who have sat with John in that prison of disillusionment, you can encounter, like John, Jesus directing your gaze away from the unmet expectations, towards the things that have been achieved. In this you will be strengthened not to take bait of offence, but will maintain your joy, knowing that "your labour in the Lord is not in vain.[20]"

There remains, however, one more question to address. Are we all chosen for ministry? And what happens when it seems that others get chosen, and we are left out? This often results in us feeling rejected and somewhat second-rate. Our last chapter, in looking at the biblical character Barsabbas, examines some of these questions.

---

19   John 3:4
20   1 Corinthians 15:58

BARSABBAS

"Who is Barsabbas?" You may ask. A quick inventory of your knowledge of biblical characters will probably draw a blank, so I must begin this chapter by introducing him and outlining why I have included this largely unknown character amongst the likes of Abraham, Paul, and John the Baptist.

You first encounter Barsabbas in Acts chapter one, and find that his name was Joseph, but he was called Barsabbas, (and also Justus.) Here you'll find that he and a man called Matthias were put forward as candidates to replace Judas Iscariot who had committed suicide after betraying Jesus. In Acts chapter one verse twenty-four the apostle's prayer is recorded.

"Then they prayed, "Lord, you know everyone's heart. Show us which of these two you have chosen to take over this apostolic ministry, which Judas left to go where he belongs."

Having cast lots, it reads,

"... the lot fell to Matthias; so, he was added to the eleven apostles."

The reason I have included Barsabbas in my study on God's call was his experience of not being chosen for the role of apostle and how he responded to this. I think many of us would have had the experience of not being chosen or seeing somebody else step into things we aspired to, or someone more successful or 'anointed' than us. Conversely, you may recall times you were chosen, and the surge of pride, confidence and affirmation that came with that.

Both these scenarios can impact on the outworking of call. To those, who experience not being affirmed, chosen or seemingly specially anointed this is often hard, and even more difficult when it appears that God is doing the choosing (as in Barsabbas' case), and we (for whatever reason) find ourselves occupying the 'unchosen' spot. When this happens, it is hard not to feel rejected and somewhat lesser than the one who was chosen.

However, for those with strong gifts and attractive qualities, the difficulty can be learning that these things don't hold currency in God's evaluation of people's worth. Jesus tells an interesting parable that reflects somewhat on this topic. Matthew twenty, records the parable of the workers in the vineyard. In it, a landowner goes out early in the morning to hire labourers to work in his vineyard. Later, he goes out and finds others in the marketplace who had not been hired, so he hires them also. He does this again at the sixth hour, the ninth hour and the eleventh hour.

It is interesting to pause at this point and ponder why these men were still in the marketplace. The obvious reason is that they had not been chosen by others to be hired. And so, he hires them. Now, in my reckoning, normally, the strongest and most desirable people get chosen first not unlike children choosing who will be on their sports team. Thus, as the day progresses the people left are increasingly the less desirable, the unchosen. By the time you get to the eleventh hour, you are down to the dregs. They have been at the market all day, and no one has chosen them. I imagine these may have had some aspects of age, or ability that made them less-desirable prospects for employment. Yet here comes the landowner, and he employs them.

At the end of the day, the parable takes a dramatic turn. They all line up to receive their pay, and those who were employed last (the least desirables) are paid first, but not only this, they are paid for the full day. Seeing this, those who were employed earlier expected that they would be paid more, but when they are paid the same amount, they begin to get angry. Why? Was it because they didn't get paid what was agreed? No, they had agreed to work the day for a denarius, the reason they were angry was that the landowner had made them equal with those who, because they were not chosen earlier, worked less time.

Their anger perhaps stems from being unhappy that those 'unchosen ones,' who everyone else rejected, were being valued at the same rate as they were. Their self-image and expectations were bound up with their ability to produce. Yet the landowner runs roughshod over this by valuing those who were not chosen, and less productive, at the same level as they.

Jesus, in telling this parable, is giving us a window into what the Kingdom of Heaven is like. God is the landowner who draws into his workforce those others often reject, the 'unchosen.' Not only this, but he values them at the same level of those who come, full of gifts and strength. We may not like it when God elevates the less desirable and values them the at the same level as us. We may even be offended that he is not as impressed with our gifts and strength as we are. But this is how God runs His Kingdom.

Having seen the effect on those who were chosen

first, let's look now at the possible impact on those who were employed later. The parable records the reaction of the workers who were first employed, but not of those who were employed later, I imagine that they would have been surprised, but then also healed to a degree of the shame and pain of not being chosen.

I have seen this happen. The healing effect of inclusion and value to those who have only known rejection and exclusion. Jean Vanier who pioneered the L'Arche communities for the handicapped wrote

"The belief in the inner beauty of each human being is at the heart of L'Arche, at the heart of all true education and at the heart of becoming human.[1]"

Those who came later would have expected less pay, but now they can now come home and feed their families, having felt the emotional warmth of having been valued and included.

It may also have had an impact on the way they saw the future. If this landowner (who was an important person) was going to continue to operate this way, then the fear and anxiety they felt each day when they arrived at the marketplace would now be eased. The fear of missing out if they were not chosen would be abated, knowing that if they were chosen now, or later, they would still be provided for.

If Barsabbas' had adopted this Kingdom view,

---

1   Becoming Human, Jean Vanier, Paulist Press, New York, 23

then he would be able to receive not being chosen as the apostle to replace Judas peacefully, knowing that he is still loved, and that he would be chosen at some point further down the track. In submitting to this decision, he would know that God's love and value on his life is not at stake.

To not have this view results in both pride and competition. Pride causes you to look down on those less gifted or strong as you are. Inwardly you can think that God is impressed with your gifts and values you above others. On the other hand, when competition rules, you will see others as a threat and compete with them for positions which will strengthen your ego and sense of self-worth. From here, any rejection, is received as a negative statement regarding your own value. You become blind to the possibility that there can be multiple reasons for selecting the other person for that position that may have nothing to do with you, and certainly have no bearing on your value and worth before God.

It seems that Barsabbas was secure in his value before God and this is seen by his on-going relationship with the church. Had he been insecure, the rejection would have perhaps caused him to withdraw himself and punish the church (and maybe God) for the pain he felt. Instead, you read in Acts fifteen verse twenty-two that Barsabbas continued to function as leader to the church in Jerusalem, and because of this, he was chosen by the church to accompany Paul and Barnabas back to Antioch to relay the letter written from the Jerusalem council regarding the Christian position on the requirements of Jewish law on Christians.

Like the men chosen later in the parable, Barsabbas whilst not initially chosen to join the apostles, is chosen later for this important task. The Greek word *apostolos* which in English is apostle, literally means 'one who is sent.' Barsabbas being sent by the church in Jerusalem has now stepped into the apostle role (one who is sent), in the company of Paul and Barnabas, and Silas who all operated in apostolic roles.

The fact that he joined later makes no difference to his value, nor his reward. The purposes of him not being chosen initially, lay in the sovereign mystery of God's will. However, had Barsabbas been insecure, and not at peace in his own value in God's eyes, he may have forfeited, or delayed walking in his call.

Conclusion

Interacting with Barsabbas' journey alerts us to our need to embrace God's Kingdom values in the outworking of our own call, so that we can see the ways that God is including and valuing all people. In doing this, we are enabled to see ourselves correctly, as well as value and dignify those that others may not choose because they are not strong or outwardly capable or attractive. Paul in this first letter to the Corinthians, in chapter two wrote,

"Brothers think of what you were when you were called. Not many of you were wise by human standards; not many of you were influential; not many of you were of noble birth. But God chose the foolish things of the world to shame the wise; God chose the weak things of this world to shame the strong. He chose the lowly things of this world and the despised things—and the things that are not-to nullify the things that are, so that no one may boast before Him."

The fact that Paul says, 'not many were influential, or of noble birth,' means that some were. But these who were, could not boast before God about these things. Conversely, those that were not chosen by the world for influence or power, needed to know that they too were valuable, and chosen by God for the work of His Kingdom.

I personally have been significantly ministered to, by those the world would overlook, the unchosen of the world. So often they have been my teachers, the means of wisdom, humility and grace. They helped me get over being too impressed with myself and my gifts, and slowly realise that the Kingdom of heaven works on an entirely different value system than this world.

Perhaps this is what Jesus meant in Matthew twenty, verse sixteen when He said,

"So, the last will be first, and the first will be last."

ART GALLERIES, WALKING TRACKS AND JIGSAW PUZZLES

As I bring this book into land, all that is left to do is to turn back to look at the metaphors I mentioned in the introduction. These are intended to give you, the reader, some context of meaning by which to understand the journey you have been on.

The first metaphor I mentioned was that of an art gallery. On my last trip to Italy, during some time in Florence, I was able to visit the Uffizi Art Gallery. It was to me a great experience, as I walked through rooms and rooms of exquisite art pieces. In like manner, we have walked down a corridor on which have been hung pictures depicting the lives of Abram, Joseph, Martha and all the other people whose lives I have written on in this book.

The purpose of looking into their stories, the art of their lives, is not so much to see them, but see ourselves reflected in them and come away changed.

Edward Robinson in his book, *The Language of Mystery* wrote,

"There is a generosity about true works of art. They give to us what we wish to take, all we feel we can use, free and for nothing.[1]"

Earlier I quoted Ephesians two verse ten that says we are God's workmanship. The Greek word for workmanship is *poema,* and some have translated this as 'works of art.' In looking at God's work in the lives of the various people we have examined, God is at work in our lives, in the interaction between art and the viewer. Edward Robinson says this is,

"The alchemy that turns matter into spirit.[2]"

He says,

"Released by my own imaginative openness into this new dimension I am set free to discover more of myself; to explore the same ocean which touches us all, but particularly to discover what is of special significance to me as a person.[3]"

The great thing is that we are not passive in this process, but we are co-labourers with God in the generation of this art. Edward Robinson wrote,

---

1   Edward Robinson, The Language of Mystery, Trinity Press International, Philadelphia, 1987, 38
2   Ibid., 38
3   Ibid., 38-39

"We know a poet, wrote Coleridge, because he makes us poets.[4]"

And so, the creative hand of God brings to life our creativity, to work with Him on the work of art which is our lives. Richard Wurmbrand, who was imprisoned in Romania under the communist regime, in one of his sermons from solitary confinement wrote,

"I know my duty. It does not so much consist in doing things. Prison conditions hinder me from accomplishing deeds. Duty consists mostly in becoming something. 'I am what I am' is the usual translation of what God said to Moses. A more literal rendering of the Hebrew *'Ehjeh asher ehjah'* is, 'I will become what I will become'. He Himself is constantly becoming something. This is my duty too.[5]"

As we have wandered together down the art gallery of the Bible, looking with care at the works of art of Joseph, Paul, Barsabbas and others, the interaction of the Holy Spirit brings alive the formation of our own lives, and draws us towards our duty of co-labouring with God in the creation of what we are becoming.

The second metaphor I used was a walking track. In our years of living in Canada, the snowy winters precluded many people from walking outside.

---

4   Ibid., 38 -39
5   Richard Wurmbrand, Sermons in Solitary Confinement, Hodder and Stoughton, London, 1969, 44

Thus, in the town we lived, they had built a big indoor recreation centre, which included an indoor walking track. My wife and I made good use of this over the winter months.

The purpose then of a walking track was not that it takes you to a destination, but that in the walking (or running) of it, you become fitter through the process. In like manner, the road we have travelled in this book is not intended to bring you to a specific destination, but it serves the purpose that in the walking of it, you have become fitter and strengthened for the purposes God has before you.

The apostle Paul in writing his second letter to his disciple Timothy wrote "I have finished the race.[6]"

Similarly, in his letter to the believers in Corinth, he wrote,

"Do you not know that in a race, all the runners run, but only one gets the prize. Run in such a way to get the prize.[7]"

No runner hoping to win, does not engage in training. And so, the purpose of this book was to provide a road by which you might train, and in doing so be strengthened for the running of your race.

The final metaphor I mentioned was that of a jigsaw puzzle. In this metaphor you yourself are the piece of the puzzle, and the puzzle provides the context of meaning for your life. In a conversation I had

6   2 Timothy 4:7
7   1 Corinthians 9:24

recently, someone wondered out loud to me about the complexity and scope of the lives of billions of people on earth, and what ultimately is the meaning of it all. This metaphor speaks to this question.

With a jigsaw each piece is not the picture but is part of the picture. In it, we understand that each piece is uniquely shaped to create a larger picture, of which it is only a part. In like manner, you are uniquely made and shaped by the hand of God, to fit into the time and place of your life. The perimeter of your piece touches only a limited number of other pieces, but as each does its part, the larger picture is created.

In this way you are a piece of art, within a larger piece of art that God is constructing over time and history. Its complexity and scope are beyond our imagination. This is why the apostle Paul wrote,

"Now to Him who is able to do immeasurably more than all we ask or imagine, according to His power that is at work within us.[8]"

The final work of God will be far beyond what we can imagine, and our piece of the puzzle will only be fully understood when we see it in the context of the completed picture. In this way, the full realisation of this will not happen in our short lifetime. But for now, the power of God is at work within you, working with you to shape and develop your life that you

---

8   Ephesians 3:20

might become what you will become, and God calls you to work with Him in this noble task.

My prayer is that as we have walked the art gallery together, that God's alchemy has brought you gold to enrich your life. That in running the track together, you are fitter and stronger for the running of your race. That in looking at your piece of the puzzle, you have glimpsed that you are a work of art, within a larger work that will ultimately display the manifold wisdom of God to all the authorities in the heavenly realm,[9] to the glory of God forever and ever. Amen.

---

9   Ephesians 3:10

Colin founded WORDS OF LIFE ministries that provides resources, teaching and training for churches to assist building people up to maturity in Christ.

For more info visit www.wolnz.org or email colin.shilston@gmail.com